My First Diwali
Baby Book – High Contrast
0-12 Months

Test page

Diwali

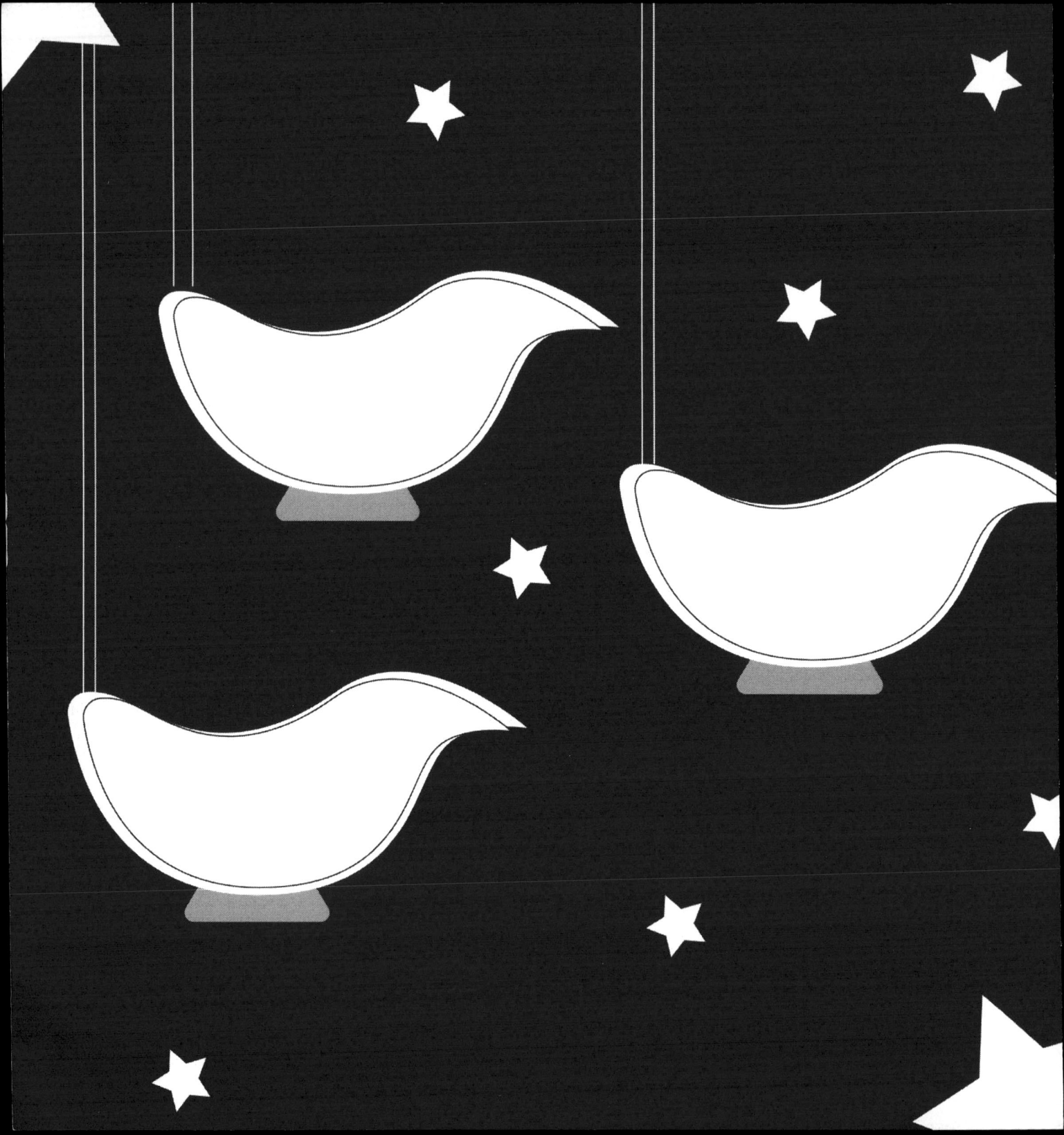

Diwali

Our team worked very hard to prepare for You this product. We would be very pleased if you leave your opinion as it will help us develop further.

Thank you

Printed in Great Britain
by Amazon